Making Leather Gear

by

Daddy Wendell

To my boy Hobbit for all her support.

INTRODUCTION

Imagine visiting your favorite leather / fetish shop - you walk through the door and, as your eyes adjust to the light, your sense of smell is overwhelmed by the scent of leather. After you adjust, you see the twinkle of brass and nickel hardware and the shine of patent leather; the deep black of oil tanned leather makes the colored piping and accents stand out like neon.

If you read any further, that magic will be ruined. Your next visit to the shop will be spent examining every piece of gear – you'll scrutinize it, deconstruct it, know exactly how it was made and possibly even how you could improve on it.

Prior to the advent of stores selling leather gear in the 1960s, gear had to be custom made or purchased from a variety of sources (motorcycle gear, equestrian gear, and medical restraints, to name a few) and potentially required extensive modification after purchase. Most of the iconic pieces of leather gear featured in illustrations by Tom of Finland or in photos in Drummer magazine come from motorcycle gear or modified equestrian equipment.

In the late 1960s, leather shops began opening in the "gay ghetto" of major cities. Operating on a small budget (and even smaller space) many shops would resell motorcycle leathers and their own custom-made pieces of gear. Industrial sewing machines are expensive, loud, and take up space. If a shop could not afford the money and space for a sewing machine, they would purchase their sewn leather gear from another source for resale. The alternative, sewing leather by hand, is a time consuming and laborious process.

Leather gear from the '60s and '70s was often made with harness thickness leather which required time and wear to "break in." This need to "break in" gear was a laborious and potentially painful process. The owner had to spend a significant amount of time and effort applying leather conditioner and polish and wearing a piece of gear to stretch it and soften the edges before it could be worn regularly.

As the industry matured in the late-1970s, leather workers began making straps with a new technique: using garment thickness or upholstery thickness leather, they folded it in half, glued it and sewed along the edges to create a supple, rounded edge leather strap. This made gear more comfortable and affordable because the leather was already soft, required no time or effort to break it in, and garment or upholstery leather, even doubled, is considerably less expensive than harness leather.

I got my start making leather gear when I had to repair a set of cuffs that had been made in the early 1980s. The experience piqued my curiosity and I started researching the pieces and patterns of gear that were made prior to 1980. I started by making copies of the bondage cuffs that I had repaired, then chest harnesses and belts.

When my partner won an international leather title, we needed to raise money to cover travel expenses. I pulled together a list of the pieces that I did best and offered them for sale. The first email said, "It's like buying cookies to send me to scout camp, only you're buying leather gear and sending me to Folsom Europe ... We're offering basic gear at basic prices, but it's all custom fit - instead of getting a size XL, you're getting a size 37½." It took only a few weeks of part-time work to sell enough gear to purchase a round-trip ticket from Seattle to Berlin.

All of the gear in this book can be made without a sewing machine and with a minimal set of tools that fit inside a book bag. If you make your own gear, you can save a considerable amount of money – a piece of gear that sells for $120 in a leather store would take an hour and $20 worth of leather and hardware to make.

My friend Ash spent the Folsom Street Fair weekend helping me make and sell leather gear. On Sunday afternoon, as we were packing up and counted the money, she said, "It's really not that difficult. Almost everything that you did today, I learned in leather crafts class at scout camp."

Imagine the sense of pride that you will feel when you give someone a piece of gear and say, "I made this." Imagine their pride wearing a piece of gear that you made especially for them. You can also customize the gear to the person – design, color and a perfect fit.

Leather

You can find leather from almost any animal: deer, pig, goat, cow, bull, buffalo, reptile, even fish! If it has a hide, someone has probably made leather out of it.

A piece of leather is described by its "weight" or thickness; one ounce is equal to 1/64th of an inch thickness. Ounces is also used as an abbreviation of ounces per square foot. Leather described as having a weight of 7 to 8 oz. means the leather is 7/64th to 8/64th of an inch thickness and a square foot of the leather should weigh 7 to 8 ounces. This weight may vary depending on the density of the leather.

Variations in the hide cause leather to be described with a range of thickness, such as 4 to 5 ounce. Leathers of certain thickness are also described by name, e.g. Garment leather is 1.5-3 oz, Upholstery leather is 2.5-4 oz, Chap leather is 3-5.5 oz, Belt or Strap leather is 6-12 oz.

Tannin, extracted from the bark of oak trees, was originally used to process leather, hence the term, "Tanning." Hides processed using tannin are called "Vegetable tanned." Hides processed using chromium salts are called, "Chrome tanned."

"Vegetable tanned" hides are usually top grain with no additional oils added. The finish is smooth, slick, light brown in color and can usually be polished with wax products. If it gets wet, it will darken in color, shrink and harden as it dries.

"Chrome Tanned" leather is more supple than vegetable tanned leather and can have a smooth, slick surface or a soft, supple surface depending on the final finish. Chrome tanned leathers are dyed during the tanning process and are usually polished with wax.

"Retanned leather" is vegetable tanned leather that has then been chrome tanned to make the leather more water resistant.

"Oil Tanned" is a misnomer - oils are worked into the (usually chrome tanned) leather at the end of the tanning process. The oils provide protection and a matte finish. "Oil tanned" leather will feel oily, greasy or even waxy and should not be polished with wax or cream finishes.

"Patent leather" is chrome tanned leather that has had an artificial finish applied after the tanning process. Polishing patent leather can be problematic because each type has different care instructions.

After tanning, a hide may be "split." Splitting is the process of separating a hide into two or more layers - each layer is called a split. A hide that is not split is called "Full Grain" because the outer layer of the hide (the grain) is left on and only the hair has been removed. Each split can be sanded to produce a suede finish or embossed with a design and finished. Splitting is used to give a hide a more consistent thickness. A hide that ranges from 8-16oz can be split and trimmed into multiple 4oz hides that have very consistent thickness. The topmost split is called "Top Grain" because it has the outer layer of the hide (the grain) on it. Top Grain may be sanded to remove scars and then treated to cover the work.

Leather may be "vat dyed" or "surface dyed." Vat dyed leather will be the same color on both sides and surface dyed leather will be different colors on each side. Vat dyed leather will be more expensive but it will have more consistent color because the hide is immersed in the dye solution. The finish applied on top of the dye may dramatically change the leather color and the texture – for example, the finished shide is a shiny, dark hunter green while the unfinished side is a pale mint green.

HARDWARE

left to right: Strap buckle, roller buckle (with keeper above), D ring, O ring, Scissor Snap, Bolt Snap.

Buckles

The "body" of the buckle holds the components of the buckle together. The tongue is the center part of the buckle that goes through the hole in the strap. Some buckles have an optional "roller" (both buckles shown above are "roller buckles.") A keeper may be used to hold the strap down. The Strap buckle (also known as a "center bar" buckle) has an integral keeper.

Rings

Rings are used for joining straps together and come in a variety of shapes and sizes. Pictured above are the D ring and the O ring.

Clips

Pictured above are the scissor clip, used as a retaining clip, and the bolt clip, often used on leashes. The scissor clip may release under tension, while the bolt clip will not.

Pressed versus Welded Hardware

Pressed hardware is made from metal that is pressed together, leaving a small gap between the ends. Small, inexpensive O and D rings are usually made with pressed hardware. "Welded hardware" is hardware which has the ends welded to keep them from separating. Welded hardware should always be used where a load is placed on the hardware, because pressed hardware will separate under tension, causing potentially dangerous conditions.

Pressed metal D ring pulled apart, welded ring D held together.

LEATHER AND HARDWARE SOURCES

There are two primary sources for equipment and materials: Tandy Leather and your local commercial leather shop, in Seattle, MacPherson Leather; Portland, the Oregon Leather Company; San Francisco, Hide House (located in Napa, California.)

Tandy Leather is a nationwide franchise of retail stores geared toward the leather working hobbyist. They are a small, locally run store, they may offer classes in leather working techniques and the staff is usually knowledgeable and helpful. Their selection will be smaller and the prices more expensive than the commercial leather shop and they tend to cater toward people doing leather carving or embossing.

An internet search or phone book search for upholstery supplies, saddle making supplies and/or leather hides should help locate local commercial sources for supplies and equipment.

Your local commercial leather shop may sell leather to saddle makers, upholsterers and anyone else in your area who works with leather. Some shops may specialize, for example a store that sells only upholstery leather. The staff will be busy and may not have the breadth of knowledge to answer specific questions about leather working – the person who specializes in handling upholstery accounts may not know much about leather for strapping, for example. It is unlikely that a commercial leather store will offer classes.

Prices will be less expensive at commercial leather stores; however they may have purchase restrictions, a minimum dollar amount per order, require you to have a business license to shop at their store or sell bulk quantities (e.g. whole hides, 100 packs of hardware etc.). One way around the "whole hide" issue is to ask if they have a scrap bin.

THE SCRAP BIN

The scrap bin at large leather stores is an excellent resource for pieces of leather that can be used for small projects. Many stores sell scrap leather by the pound or at a discount and you can find some great bargains in the scrap bin - larger stores will have multiple scrap areas, e.g. strap leather, upholstery leather, garment leather, etc. Ask when they put new additions into the scrap bin - some shops may have specific times that they add new items.

"Surfing" is checking the top of the bin(s) for new additions. "Diving" is working your way through the whole bin. Wear work gloves to protect against sharp edges and sharp objects that may get into the scraps and examine the contents of the whole bin. While this can be time consuming, a thorough "dive" will likely find a buried treasure that "surfers" miss.

If you don't have a lot of time, make a quick surf of the scrap bin; you may find something that was just dropped into the scrap bin or that was churned up by a "diver."

If you find a piece that looks good, examine it carefully to see why it was discarded. Look for flaws in finish, texture, thickness and color - nicks, scratches, thin/thick spots, stiff/flexible spots.

Consider the lighting and color of the leather - the fluorescent lights you usually find in a leather shop may cause the leather to appear different than it will in natural light - if possible, examine the leather under natural light. Dim lighting in clubs and bars will mute colors - creating a piece that appears bright red in a dimly lit club may require an almost-pink piece of leather. Similarly, black lights in clubs and bars may cause some dyes to fluoresce with unintended colors.

Another source to consider is the "exotic leather" scrap bin – while the price per pound may appear astronomical, reptile and other exotic leather hides tend to be thin, so 1/4 pound can be a lot of leather. Exotic leather scraps can be used to make unique small pieces or as accents on less expensive larger leather pieces, e.g. stingray wrist bands, ostrich bicep bands, snakeskin flogger handles.

Most of the leather gear described in this book is designed to be made using 6-12 oz strap leather in either wax finish or oil finish. A large piece of strap leather would be a good investment as your first leather purchase.

TOOLS

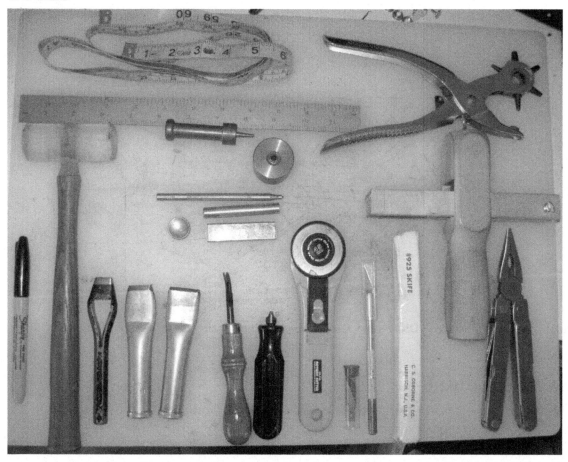

A basic set of tools - from left to right: (top) Measuring tape, metal ruler, rotary hole punch. (middle, below ruler) OO Grommet setter, snap setter and anvil, rivet setter and anvil. (bottom) Marking Pen, Mallet, ½" punch, ¾" punch, 1" punch, edge beveller, screwdriver, rotary cutter, X-Acto knife and blades, Skife (in box), strap cutter, Leatherman multi-tool.

BASIC TOOLS

The best way to put together a set of leather working tools is to purchase quality tools individually. The sets of "leather working" tools sold by leather hobby shops are intended for people doing leather tooling (leather engraving) and contain many tools that are not used in making leather gear. The tools also tend to be inexpensive and will wear out quickly.

Many pieces of leather gear can be made with nothing more than a cutting board, metal ruler, single-edged razor blade and a rotary punch.

CUTTING BOARD

Get the biggest cutting board you can afford. Commercial kitchen supply stores are the best places to get them. I have a small cutting board (4"x6") that I use when I travel and a large cutting board (2'x3') for the workshop at home.

CUTTING TOOLS

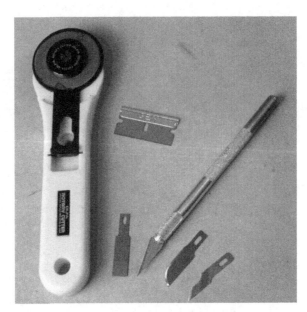

Basic cutting tools - left to right: Olfa rotary cutter, single-edged razor blade, X-Acto knife and blades.

Single-edge razor blade

This is your least expensive option and very useful for fine detail work. Your fingers will get tired and sore after a few hours of using it as your primary cutting tool.

Hobby knife or utility knife

I've seen some incredible leather work has been done with these very basic cutting tools. A Hobby knife (the trademarked name is "X-Acto knife") uses a blade that's equivalent to a single-edged razor blade. A utility knife (also known as a "box cutter") uses a thicker disposable blade that lasts longer, but the blade thickness can make it difficult to do fine detail work.

Rotary cutter

This is essentially a round, single-edge razor blade on a stick. It works very well for cutting all thicknesses of leather and, when used with a metal edged ruler, makes excellent straight cuts – ideal for cutting straps and flogger falls.

STRAP AND STRIP CUTTING TOOLS

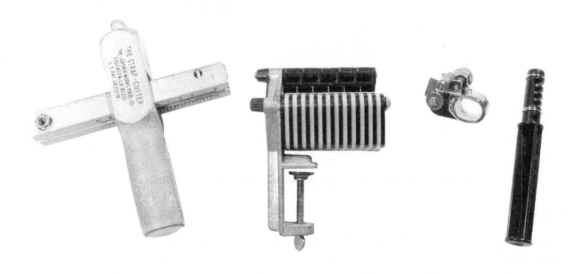

Strap, strip and lace cutting tools - left to right: Strap cutter, "Jerry Stripper" strip cutter, "Australian Strander" and a "Craftool Lace Maker."

Strap Cutter and Australian Strander

These tools work by pulling them along the edge of a hide. Whenever possible, cut straps down the length of a hide rather than across the width of the hide, because leather cut from the length of the hide has consistent thickness and flexibility, while straps cut from across the width of the hide will be shorter and have thickness and flexibility vary to such a degree that they will not give good results.

Thin, supple, or flexible leathers can be difficult to cut into strips because the leather flexes or stretches as it goes through the cutter, causing variations in the width of the strap. To minimize variations in width, carefully set the inside height of the tool (wide enough to minimize drag and narrow enough to block flexing) and use sharp, fresh blades.

For the best results when cutting leather into strips, use a rotary cutter and a metal straight edge. While this is time consuming, it generates the most consistent width.

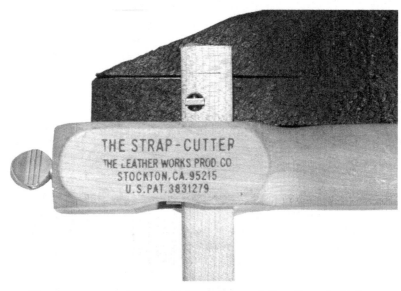

The strap cutter is pulled along the straight edge of a hide.

Strip Cutter

This cuts multiple strips with one pass. Pulling the edge of a wide hide through the strip cutter can be quite difficult. The strip cutter works best when you are breaking a thicker strap down into smaller straps, e.g. a 3" strap into four 3/4" straps. Supple leathers do not produce good results because they stretch under tension and will produce strips that are of varying width.

Strap and Strip Cutting

This hide was strapped from the top down. The top left edge was trimmed to make a straight edge, then 4 straps were cut, then the top right edge was trimmed and the fifth strap was cut.

There are two primary methods of cutting leather straps from a hide or, "strapping a hide." The first is to use a metal ruler and a cutting tool (razor, knife or rotary cutter) to cut individual straps. While this process is very time consuming, it produces the best results.

The second method of strapping a hide is to use a strap cutter. Prepare the hide by using a metal ruler and cutting tool to make a straight edge along one side of the hide. Set the strap cutter to the desired width and then pull it down the length of the hide.

Using a rotary cutter and metal ruler to cut a straight edge along the edge of the hide.

Pulling the strap cutter along the straight edge of a piece of leather to make a strap.

If you want to make a lot of thin straps, consider using the strap cutter to cut wide straps (3"-4") then using the stripper to cut the wide strap into the desired width.

Strip Cutter

This cuts multiple strips with one pass. Pulling the edge of a wide hide through the strip cutter can be quite difficult. The strip cutter works best when you are breaking a thicker strap down into smaller straps, e.g. a 3" strap into four 3/4" straps. Supple leathers do not produce good results because they stretch under tension and create strips of varying width.

Lace Cutter

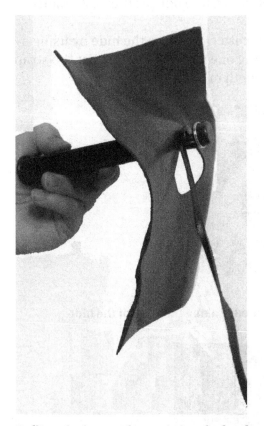

Pulling the lace and permitting the leather scrap to rotate around the cutter gives the best results when using the lace cutter.

The lace cutter is used to convert scrap leather into laces. Cut a 1" diameter circle in the center of a piece of leather; insert the lace cutter into the hole, then pull it against the inside edge of the hole to start cutting a lace. Once the lace is started, hold the lace cutter in one hand and pull on the lace with the other hand.

A 6"x6" piece of leather yields a little over 12 feet of ¼" lace using a lace cutter.

The Australian Strander can also be used in an identical manner to cut laces.

HOLE MAKING TOOLS

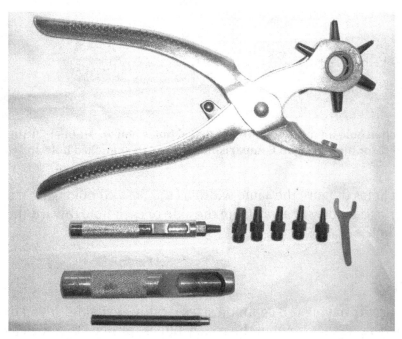

From top to bottom: rotary hole punch, screw in punch set, hole punch with "ejector hole" and inexpensive tube punch.

Punches

Punches that eject the leather scraps are preferable to the punches that are a tube with one end sharpened. Tubular punches require that the leather "holes" must be pushed or pried out before the punch fills up.

Round Punch

A round punch is used for punching holes in leather. A Number 0 punch is 5/64" diameter, and the size increases by 1/64" thereafter until the #8 punch, when it increases by 1/32" for each size.

The #6 punch is used for punching holes for Chicago Screws.

Size	0	1	2	3	4	5	6	7	8	9	10
Diameter	5/64"	3/32"	7/64"	1/8"	5/32"	11/64"	3/16"	13/64"	1/4"	9/32"	5/16"

Making an Oblong Hole with a Round Punch

Left: Oblong punched hole on top, two round punched holes below. Middle: Cutting between holes with single edged razor blade. Right: Comparison between the punched hole and the hand cut hole.

Punch two round holes that are the same width as the desired oblong hole and, using a metal edged ruler as a guide, cut away from the side of each hole toward the middle to create an oblong hole.

Rotary Punch

A rotary punch permits having 6-8 common sizes readily available. If you don't have the grip strength, need a size that is not in the rotary punch, or need to punch a hole that is not on the edge of a piece of leather, you will need to use a standard round punch. Inexpensive rotary punches generally have punch tubes that are not replaceable; more expensive punches have replaceable punch tubes.

A rotary punch can only punch holes within a few inches of the edge of a piece of leather. A rotary punch makes considerably less noise than a standard hole punch which must be pounded through the leather with a mallet.

A Rotary punch can also be used to clamp two pieces of strap together to ensure that the hole is aligned through both pieces.

Using a rotary punch to put a hole through a folded leather strap

Oblong, Oval, Rectangular and Bag Punches

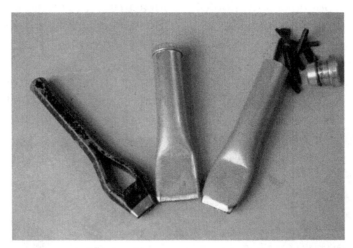

From left to right: forged ½" punch, stamped sheet metal 1" rectangular punch,

¾" oval punch with cap removed to show scrap removal.

These punches come in a variety of sizes, shapes and prices. Rectangular, oval and oblong are available in a variety of lengths and widths. Forged steel are more expensive than the stamped sheet steel. The ½" punch on the left ejects the punched pieces of leather. The two hollow punches on the right must be emptied periodically by removing the cap at the top and removing the pieces of leather from inside.

While it may seem to save time and effort, stacking leather and trying to pound a punch through the whole stack is likely to give poor results. Multiple strikes of a punch, or even a punch that goes through in a single stroke, will cause the stack of leather to shift or stretch unless the stack of leather is held very tightly together.

The best results are obtained by punching through a single piece of leather at a time.

MALLET

Use only rubber, plastic, wood or leather mallets on punches or other leather working tools. A 3-4oz plastic mallet is the most versatile, although it may take several strikes to get through thick material. A one pound rubber mallet is quite useful for getting through heavy material, although it may provide too much power for fine work.

Do not use metal hammers because they can damage the punch. If you must use a metal hammer, wrap the head in scrap leather to pad the impact.

MEASURING TOOLS

Metal or metal-edge rulers are a crucial piece of equipment. Wooden rulers should be avoided because they will be quickly chewed up by cutting tools.

A cloth measuring tape is used to take measurements from people and for measuring curves and pieces of leather when you cannot lay them out flat.

When cutting, press down firmly on the ruler to ensure that the leather does not stretch or slide while it is being cut.

Metal Ruler, metal square, cloth measuring tape.

Press firmly down on the ruler as you are cutting and shift pressure with the cutting tool.

Grooving

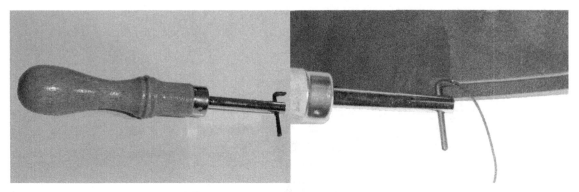

Left: Saddlemaker's Groover. Right: Groover in use.

Use a "groover" to add engraved lines parallel to the edge of a piece of leather. Adjust the arm to the desired distance from the edge and pull the groover along the edge of the leather to create a grooved line. For best results, groove the strap of leather before edging it – the sharp edge of the strap makes pulling the groover easier and gives a straight line.

Edge Beveling

Use an "edger" to bevel or round the sharp edges of freshly cut leather. Edgers come in a range of sizes, #1 is used on thin leather, #4 is used on thick leather and #2 is ideal for working 8oz leather. Push or pull or push the edger along the edge of the leather to round and soften the edge. Almost all the leather used in the projects in this book will need to be edged.

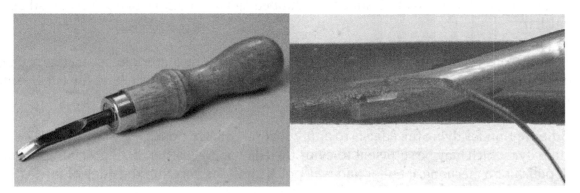

Left: Edger. Right: Edger in use.

EDGE FINISHING

Dye the edge of the leather with a cotton swab dipped in leather dye

Some leathers may not be dyed all the way through, so the edges will need to be dyed to match the surface. Using a cotton swab, wipe a single, even coat of leather dye across the edge. Allow it to dry and then check to see whether it needs another coat. If leather dye is not available, try using permanent marker. Test a sample beforehand - marker inks may produce unexpected color results on leather.

After the dye work is finished, you may oil or wax the leather (whichever is appropriate to match the finish) or use an edge slicker to "slick" or burnish the edge. An edge slicker is a piece of bone, metal, wood or plastic that is rubbed against the edge of a piece of leather to burnish it.

Gum Tragacanth (found at stores that supply leather working materials) is an edge slicking and burnishing compound that can be used to speed the process of slicking the edge. Apply a coat of it to the unfinished edge and then begin slicking the edge.

Another option for dying the edge is to apply several coats of polish – many polishes contain dye which may be sufficient to color the edge of the leather. Using a cloth saturated with polish or a mechanical buffer and wax polish, buff the wax into the edge of the leather.

Edge dressing is a product that dyes and seals the edges of leather. It is only used on the edges of boot soles and is not recommended for use on leather gear. The finish is stiff and shiny and may crack and flake if the leather is flexed.

Skiving

Skiving is shaving the back side of the leather in order to make it thinner. It is quite useful for making a belt end thinner and for making a snap end thinner in order to use a shorter snap stem.

Skife in use, shaving the edge of a leather strap to make it thinner.

Snaps

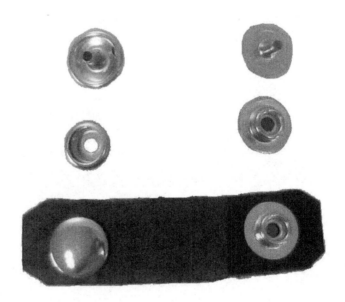

Four parts of a snap, top to bottom. Left Side: Cap, Eyelet. Right Side: Socket, Stud.

Common snap sizes are 14 (3/8"), 16 (7/16"), 18 (15/32"), 20 (1/2" diameter, 5-7 oz leather) and 24 (5/8" diameter, post should go through 8-10oz leather). Most snaps come in either short or long stem, to permit using them on thicker or thinner leather. For example, the short stem button snaps are 3/16" and long stem button snaps are 4/16"

Number	14	16	18	20	24
Cap Diameter	5/64"	7/64"	1/8"	9/64"	5/32"

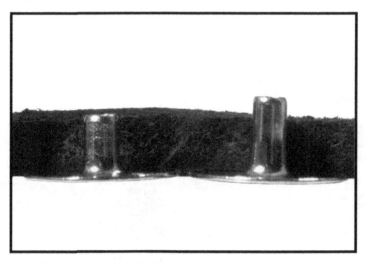

Too short stem (left) proper length stem (right.)

Cap and stud both have a stem which should be long enough to protrude through the leather and provide sufficient metal to be peened (bent over to form a rolled lip that secures the pieces together) into place by the punch. If the stem is too short, you can shave the leather down with a skife or, if the stem is too long, use a metal file to file down the stem.

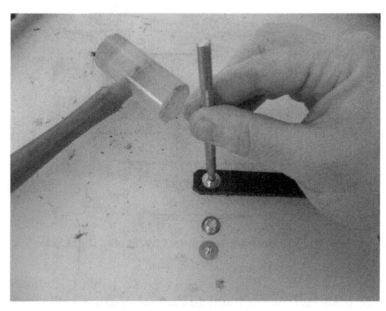

Peening a stud into place.

Punch a hole through each piece of leather, put the cap in one hole and peen the socket in place. Put the socket through the other hole and peen the stud in place.

Snaps are available with short stems and long stems, if you buy long stems, you can file them down to an appropriate length to fit through the leather you're using. If the stem is too short, your only solution is to skife the leather around the snap.

Buckle End Finish

Fold the strap over a ruler to the set the fold distance, then punch a hole through both pieces of the leather, approximately ¼ inch from the end of the strap – this technique is identical to a ring end finish. The fold distance should be enough space for the buckle and keeper and attaching hardware (rivet or Chicago screw) but not so much space that the buckle recedes into the wrap.

A fold that is too long will permit the buckle to pull back into the fold.

Center an oblong punch between the holes and punch out a slot wide enough for the buckle tongue. You may need to double-punch the tongue hole with the punch to make it wide enough for the buckle tongue. Trim any excess with an X-Acto knife.

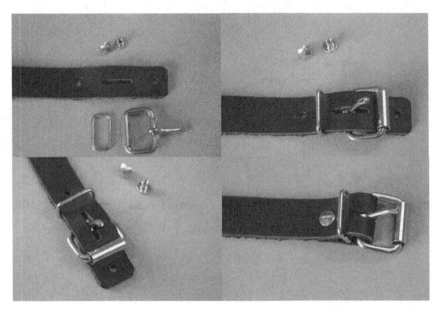

Top left: buckle end finish with tongue hole punched out. Top right: insert keeper then buckle, Bottom left: Ensure that tongue is positioned correctly. Bottom right: Fasten rivet/screw.

23

Belt End Finish

Trim the end of the belt to the desired shape – a square tip can be done with a single edged razor blade, a round tip or English Point can be done with a razor blade cutting around a template or with a punch.

For 1" width and smaller belts/straps, measure ¾" to 1" from the end and punch holes at ½" to ¾ inch intervals. For 1¼" and wider belts, measure 2 inches from the end and punch holes at 1 inch intervals. If you are making a custom fit piece of gear, plan to have the piece buckle at the second hole. The person wearing it will likely be using the third hole after the leather stretches.

Left: Completed buckle end and belt end finishes. Right: (from left to right) 1 ½" English Point Punch, English Point belt tip, Wedge Point belt tip, Square belt tip with corners clipped.

Ring End Finish

Fold the strap over the metal ruler to set the appropriate distance, then punch a hole through both pieces of the leather and attach the leather to the ring with a rivet or Chicago Screw. A 1 ½" fold works well for 1" and larger straps, however, for smaller straps, the fold can be made shorter, provided there is enough space for the ring and Chicago screw or rivet.

Left: Measure the fold. Center: Punch a hole through both pieces of leather.

Right: Attach the ring to the strap with a chicago screw or rivet.

Riveting

The two most common ways to join leather together are cap rivets or Chicago screws. Cap rivets are two pieces, a cap and a stem piece. To set a cap rivet, place the stem through a hole in both pieces of leather, place the cap on top, put one end in the anvil, cover the other end with a rivet setter and hit the setter with a mallet.

Top left (left to right): Rivet cap, rivet stem, rivet anvil, rivet setter. Bottom left, strip of leather to be riveted. Right: Setting the rivet.

Chicago Screws

Chicago screws
¼" (top) and ½" (bottom.)

Chicago Screws come in variable lengths (1/4"-3/4") but a uniform diameter – 3/16". This means that a #6 punch (3/16") is likely to be the most used punch in your toolbox.

Chicago Screws have several advantages to rivets. If a Chicago screw is secured with thread locking compound (e.g. Lock-Tite) it will be much less likely to pull apart under tension. If fastened without thread locking compound, Chicago screws can be unfastened and moved – useful in applications where something may need to be adjusted. The disadvantage to Chicago screws is that they cost 3-5 times the price of rivets.

Grommets

Left: OO Grommet in a ¾" leather strap. Middle: Grommet setter and anvil. Right: Setting a grommet.

Grommets are used to reinforce holes in leather. They can be also used as decorative accents in leather pieces. Grommets sizes are numbered and correspond to a standard hole diameter:

Number	OO	O	1	2	3	4	5
Hole Diameter	3/16"	¼"	5/16"	3/8"	7/16"	½"	5/8"

Each grommet size requires an appropriate size of grommet setter and anvil. Setting grommets is very easy – punch a hole through the leather, insert the post end of the grommet through the front and the washer over the grommet post on the back. Insert the setter through the hole in the washer and into the post and hit it with a mallet to join the two pieces of the grommet together.

Before using reinforcing grommets on a belt, verify that the buckle tongues go through the grommets. If you are using multiple buckles, verify that <u>all</u> the buckle tongues fit through the grommets. After finishing a batch of a dozen belts, I discovered that over half of the buckle tongues were too wide to fit through the grommets.

Ironing

Garment and upholstery leather can be ironed to remove (or add) creases and to stretch the leather out to a consistent thickness. Cover the ironing board with an old sheet in case the leather's dye/finish melts and runs onto the ironing board cover. Set the iron on low heat. It's best to use an iron with a Teflon finish so that it will not stick to the leather's finish.

- Iron the non-finished side of the leather.
- Do not get the leather wet, use steam, starch or sizing on the leather.
- Test a small piece of leather to ensure the heat will not damage it.

Gluing

Most leather cements smell bad and contain potentially toxic solvents, so they should be used in a well ventilated area and be careful to not get any on your skin. Nitrile gloves will block most solvents from being absorbed through your skin and will prevent glue from sticking to your skin.

To make a glued strap from garment or upholstery leather, cut a strip of leather twice the width of the strap, e.g. for a 2" width strap, you will need a 4" wide strip of leather. Using an iron set on low heat, iron the piece of leather. Mark a line down the center of the strip with a pencil (ink will eventually seep through the leather staining the finished side.)

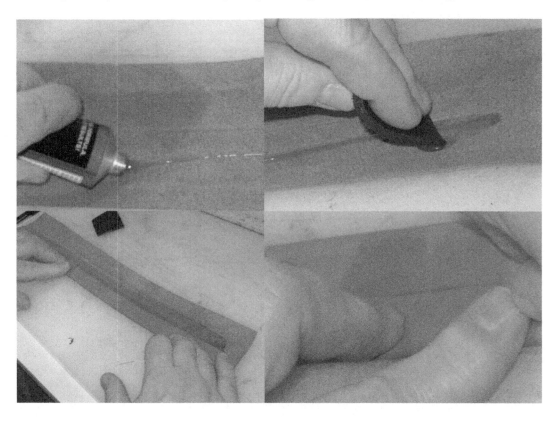

Clockwise from upper left: (1) Squeeze a line of glue between the edge of the leather and the line.
(2) Using a stiff piece of scrap leather, spread the glue across the strap piece.
(3) Working from one end of the strap to the other, fold the leather up to the center line and press into position.
(4) Repeat for the other side of the strip, folding the edge inward to meet the other edge.

After the leather has been pressed into place, wipe away any excess glue, flatten the strap with a roller or rolling pin, then clamp pieces tightly together for 12-24 hours, then put the piece in a warm place and allow remaining solvent fumes to vent for another 12-24 hours. I use C clamps and wood padded with paper towel to clamp items together.

Sewing

Garment thickness and thin upholstery leather can be sewn in a sewing machine that can handle denim. Perforations in the leather from sewing can cause the leather to rip, so it is recommended that you use a wide stitch (1/4") and a generous seam allowance to prevent the leather from ripping. Bear in mind when stitching leather that it is permanent – removing stitches leaves behind holes in the leather.

BICEP BANDS AND WRIST BANDS

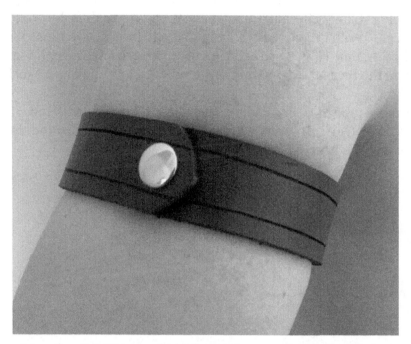

**"Why do we wear bicep bands? We wear bicep bands because they make our biceps look pretty." –
Hobbit, International Ms Leather 2008.**

Bicep bands and wrist bands are a basic piece of leather gear that are very simple to make. They can be worn for flagging – worn on the left for top, on the right for bottom; however some people wear them on both sides as decoration.

Leather

Use an 8-12oz leather, ¾" or 1" width for bicep bands, ¾" to 2" wide for wrist bands. Bicep bands and wrist bands are an excellent way to use scraps from making a belt. Cut a piece of 1 ½" width belt in half lengthwise then use the two 3/4" strips to make a pair of bicep bands that match the belt.

Hardware and Supplies

One snap per bicep band, one or two snaps for wrist bands. A single snap will work for up to 1½" width leather, wider than that will require two (or more) snaps.

Measurements

For bicep bands, have the person being measured stand with their arm **relaxed** at their side. Emphasize this strongly because many people will tense their bicep, causing the bicep band to be too large. Wrap the piece of leather above the bicep and tighten it enough to slightly compress the skin. (If you are using a tape measure, measure the same way and subtract 1/4" from the measurement.) Mark the point where the band overlaps.

For wrist bands, use a tape measure and measure around the wrist at the widest point where the band will be worn, or wrap the piece of leather loosely around the wrist and mark the point where the band overlaps.

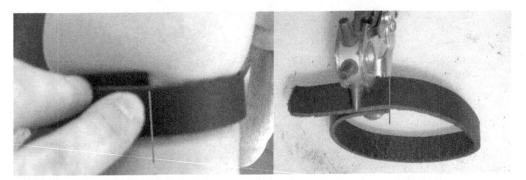

Mark the point where the band overlaps, then punch the hole(s) ½" from the overlap.

Construction

1. Wrap the band in a loop and punch a hole (through both layers of leather at the same time, if possible) for the snap 1/2" from where the band overlaps. Wrapping the band in a loop permits you to ensure that the edges of the leather align. Punching through both straps, even if the hole is slightly off center, keeps the edges of the leather aligned.
2. Groove the band (if desired.)
3. Edge the band.
4. Attach the snaps and cut the end of the band ½" – ¾" beyond the snap.

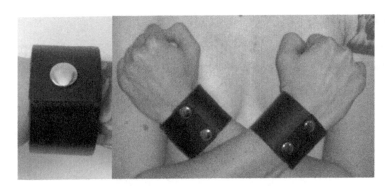

Single snap and double snap wrist bands

BASIC BELT

Recommended Leather

For a soft belt, use 6-8oz leather, for a thicker, stiffer belt, use 10-12oz harness leather. Width of the belt strap is important – dress pants have belt loops for a 1¼" wide "dress belt"; blue jeans have belt loops for a 1½" wide "sport belt"; the 2" width "garrison belt" is worn over many uniform coats and the belt loops on Utilikilts® take a 2¾" belt.

Hardware

1 buckle and keeper, same width as belt strap.
1 Chicago screw or snap.

Measurements

W = measure waist through belt loops.

Leather

1 strap (W + 6)" long.

Construction

1. Groove the belt strap (if desired.)
2. Edge the belt strap.
3. Finish the strap with a buckle end finish at one end and a belt end finish at the other end. The belt end finish should have 4-6 holes at 1" intervals starting 3" or 4" from the end of the strap.
4. Attach the buckle and keeper to the buckle end of the buckle strap, using either a snap or a Chicago screw to secure the buckle end.

SAM BROWNE BELT

One inch Sam Browne belt, worn over the right shoulder, connected with scissor clips to a single belt strap on the left hip and a two inch wide Garrison Belt worn around the waist.

Description

The Sam Browne belt was invented by Major Sam Browne of the British Army in India. He won the Victoria Cross for charging enemy gun positions during India's First War of Independence (also known as the Sepoy Mutiny or the Indian Rebellion of 1857,) but lost his right arm in the process. After his recovery, he invented what is now called, "The Sam Browne belt." This strap went over his right shoulder and held his sword in the proper location on his left hip.

The Sam Browne belt was adopted by British Indian Army officers during the 1860s. At that time, Hindu society was divided into four classes: Brahmins (teachers and priests), Kshatriyas (warriors and nobles), Vaishyas (farmers and merchants) and Shudras (servants and laborers.) In Hindu culture, the Upanayana (Sacred Thread Ceremony) is a rite of passage that is the equivalent to first communion or bar mitzvah for young men. The signifier of having completed this rite of passage is wearing the Yajnopavitam (Sacred Thread). It is tied end-to-end in a loop and, for Brahmins, worn over the left shoulder, and for Kshatriyas (the warrior class), worn over the right shoulder and attached to the left waistline.

Wearing the Sam Browne Belt over the right shoulder was a way for British Indian Army officers to signify that they belonged to the warrior class. By the turn of the century most of the world's military units had adopted the Sam Browne belt as part of their uniforms and almost all wore the belt over their right shoulder.

Materials

Use an 8-12oz harness/belt leather for the Sam Browne Belt, 1", 1¼" or 1½" work best for the Sam Browne belt. The Sam Browne Belt width should be the same as (or smaller than) the waist belt with which it is worn.

Hardware

1 buckle and keeper, 1", 1 ¼" or 1 ½".
3 Chicago screws or rivet
2 snaps and D rings, harness squares or keepers -or- 2 scissor clips.

Measurements

O = Overall Length - Measure from the top of the front left belt loop, over the right shoulder (under the epaulette, if a uniform shirt is worn) and down to the top of the rear left belt loop.
H = Buckle Height - measure from the top of the front left belt loop to the location on the chest where they want the buckle.

Leather

1 **Back strap** measures (O-H) + 4 inches (If Scissor clips are used, subtract the length of the scissor clip from the strap length.)
1 **Front strap** is H + 3 inches (If Scissor clips are to be used, subtract the length of the scissor clip from the strap length.)
1 or 2 - **Belt straps** (3x the waist belt width) – belt straps wrap around the waist belt and provide a means of attaching the Sam Browne Belt to the waist belt. One belt strap is used if two scissor clips are going to clip to a single belt strap, otherwise use two belt straps.

Construction

1. Groove all the straps (if desired.)
2. Edge all the straps.
3. Finish the **Back Strap** with a ring end finish at one end and a belt end finish at the other end, measuring 1" from the end and punching 5 holes at ¾ inch intervals.
4. Finish the **Front Strap** with a ring end finish at one end and a buckle end finish at the other end and then attach the buckle.
5. On both straps ring ends, attach a scissor clip, D ring, harness square or keeper.
6. For the (optional) **belt strap(s)**, wrap the strap around the belt that will be worn with the Sam Browne Belt and mark the overlap. Wrap the **belt strap** in a loop and punch a hole (through both layers of leather at the same time, if possible) for the snap 1/2" from where the band overlaps. Wrapping the band in a loop permits you to ensure that the edges of the leather align. Punching through both straps, even if the hole is slightly off center, keeps the edges of the leather aligned.
7. If D rings, harness squares or keepers are being used, insert a **belt straps** through each one.

Sam Browne belt with belt straps attached through D Rings.

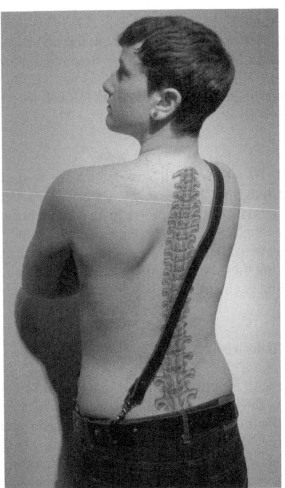

Sam Browne belt that uses Scissor Clips
to attach to a matching Bondage Belt.

BONDAGE BELT

One of the many possible uses for a bondage belt

Recommended Leather

A bondage belt should be made of fairly flexible leather, a 6-12oz harness leather is optimal.

Hardware

1 buckle and keeper, same width as belt strap
5 Chicago screws
2 D rings, O Rings or Halter Squares with an outside width that will fit through either 1¼" wide dress belt loops or 1½" wide sport belt loops.

Measurements

W = Waist, measure around the waist through the belt loops.

Leather

1 **end strap** (W - 6) inches long.
2 straps 9 inches long, called the **buckle strap** and the **middle strap**.

Note: All straps should be the same width as the inside width of the O Ring, D Ring or Halter Squares used in the bondage belt.

Bondage belt before assembly, top: end strap.

Bottom: buckle, keeper, buckle strap, ring, middle strap, ring

Construction

1. Groove all the straps (if desired.)
2. Edge all the straps.
3. Finish the **end strap** with a ring end at one end and a belt end at the other end. Punch holes at 1" intervals, starting 3" from the buckle end and going to 3" from the ring end.
4. Finish the **buckle strap** with a buckle end at one end and a ring end at the other
5. Finish the **middle strap** with ring ends at both ends.
6. Attach the buckle and keeper to the buckle end of the **buckle strap**.
7. Attach a D Ring or O ring to the ring end of the **buckle strap**.
8. Attach the **middle strap** to the other side of the **buckle strap's** ring, then attach a D Ring or O ring to the other end of the **middle strap**, then attach the ring end of the **tongue strap** to that ring.

Bondage belt after assembly.

Bondage belt looped over itself

Bondage belt with loop rings

Materials

Use an 8-12oz harness leather, the under belt should be a 1 ½" width strap and the over belt should be a 1" width strap. The belt pictured above is made with a 12oz red harness leather under belt and a 10oz black harness leather over belt.

Hardware

1 buckle and keeper, same width as belt strap.
15 Chicago screws.
5 D rings (1") or Loop Rings (shown.)

Measurements

W = Waist, measure around the waist through the belt loops.

Leather

1 **under belt** (W + 7½)" long, 1 ½" width.
1 **over belt** (W -12)" long, 1" width.

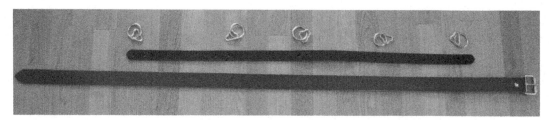

Bondage Belt before assembly – Rings (top,) over belt (middle,) under belt (bottom.)

Leather

1. Edge all the straps.
2. Finish the **under belt** with a buckle end finish at one end and a belt end finish at the other end. Starting 3" from the belt end, punch holes at 1" intervals for 6".
3. Attach the buckle to the **under belt**.

4. Measure (W/2) from the buckle end fold and mark this as the center point of the **under belt**.

5. Punch holes in the middle of the **under belt** ½" left and right of the center of the belt – this will create two holes 1" apart.

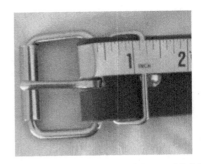

Measure from the buckle end fold.

6. Using the **over belt**, mark the **center point**, and the points 1 3/8" in from the left and right ends of the belt **(left/right end points)** then mark the points midway between the **center point** and the **left and right end points (left/right center points.)**

7. Line up the **under belt center point** mark with the **over belt center point** mark, and then mark the **left/right end points** and the **left/right center points** on the **under belt**.

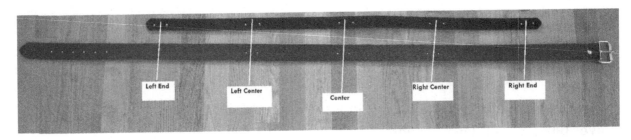

8. At each of the five marks on the **over belt**, punch holes 5/8" to the left and right of the mark – this will create two holes, 1¼" apart.

9. At each of the five marks on the **under belt**, punch holes 1/2" left and right of the mark – this will create two holes, 1" apart.

10. The extra ¼" of leather in the **over belt** will form a loop that will hold the ring in place. Use Chicago Screws to secure each ring in place.

11. After all the rings are secured in place, punch holes in the middle of the belt midway between each of the rings and screw the belts together with a Chicago Screw.

Extra leather in the over belt loops over the ring.

SUSPENDERS

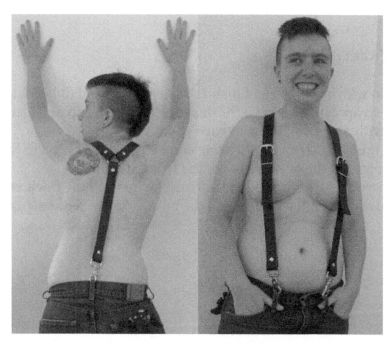

Parker proudly showing off a new pair of 1" width suspenders.

Recommended Leather

Use a 6-12oz harness/belt leather and 1" or 1 ¼" straps. These suspenders are fairly simple to make. Preparing the straps in advance (with the ring ends of each strap unfinished) and packaging all the materials together it's possible to have suspender "kits" packaged in advance and be able to finish off a pair of suspenders in a few minutes.

Parker spent the weekend helping us setup and run a play party and stayed to help clean up after Sunday brunch. I made this set of suspenders for Parker as a thank you gift for all the hard work over the weekend.

Hardware

2 buckles and keepers, the same width as the strap
8 Chicago screws or rivets
3 Scissor clips
1 D ring with an inside width that matches the strap width (i.e. 1" strap = 1" inside width D Ring); an O
   Ring with a diameter twice the strap width (i.e. if using 1" strap, use a 2" O ring) or a harness ring.

Measurements

H = measure from the top of front left belt loop to the location on the chest where you want the buckle.
B = measure from the top of the rear center belt loop to the location of the ring in the back.
S = measure over the shoulder from the location of the ring in the back to the location on the chest where they want the buckle.
L = length of a scissor clip.

Leather

2 **front straps**, (H + 1.5) - L inches long.

2 **shoulder straps**, S + 4 inches long.
1 **back strap**, (B + 1.5) - L inches long.

Construction

1. Groove all the straps (if desired.)
2. Edge all the straps.
3. Finish each **front strap** with a buckle end finish at one end, ring end finish at the other.
4. Finish each **shoulder strap** with a belt end finish at one end, ring end finish at the other.
5. Finish the back strap with a ring end finish at each end.
6. Attach the ring end of the **back strap** and the ring end of the **front straps** to the O ring.
7. Attach buckles and keepers to the buckle ends of the **front straps**.
8. Attach one scissor clip to the each ring end of the **front straps** and the **back strap**.
9. Buckle the belt ends of the **shoulder straps** into the buckles in the **front straps**.

ANKLE OR WRIST BONDAGE CUFFS

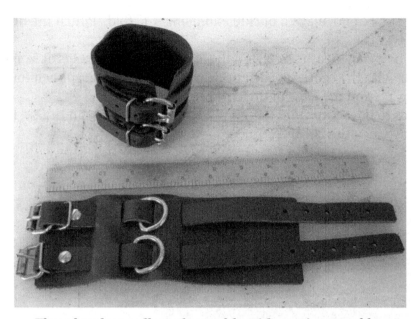

These bondage cuffs can be used for either wrists or ankles.

These bondage cuffs are fairly simple to make, flexible and have no metal hardware touching skin. Many of the single strap cuff designs will slip under tension – these cuffs are much less likely to slip because they use two straps and both straps are looped through the cuff.

Hardware

4 buckles and keepers, ¾".
4 D rings, ¾" inside diameter.
4 Chicago Screws or rivets.

Leather

Use a 6-8oz supple leather for the cuffs and either the same or a contrasting color/texture leather of similar thickness and flexibility for the straps.

2 **cuff pieces**, 3"x9" for wrist cuffs; for ankle cuffs use 3"x11" pieces.
4 **straps**, ¾"x13" for wrist cuffs; for ankle cuffs use 14-16" length straps.

Cuff pieces may be made shorter or longer, depending on the size of the person. The **straps** should be 3-5" longer than the **cuff pieces**.

Construction

1. Edge all the leather pieces.
2. For each **strap's** buckle end, make a buckle end using a 1" fold. Punch the buckle tongue hole with a ½" punch.
3. For each **strap's** belt end, measure 1" from the end and punch 5 holes at ¾ inch intervals.
4. Using a ¾" punch, with the center of each punch ¾" from the edge, punch four holes at 1" intervals, starting 2" from the edge of the **cuff piece**.
5. Attach the buckles to the **straps** and then thread each strap through the ¾" holes in the cuff. Thread a D ring between the 2nd and 3rd hole.
6.

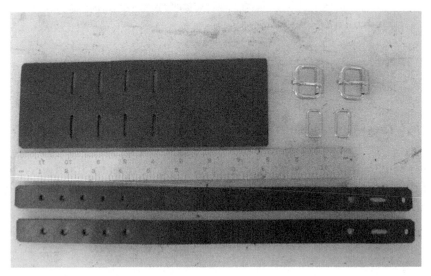

Cuffs before assembly – cuff and hardware (top,) straps (bottom.)

SIMPLE HOGTIE

Simple Hogtie with wrist and ankle cuffs

Recommended Leather

Use an 8-12oz harness/belt leather and 1" or 1 ¼" straps.

Hardware

5 Chicago Screws
4 Scissor clips

Leather

2 –**straps**, 24 inches long.

Construction

1. Groove both straps (if desired.)
2. Edge both straps and punch a hole in the center of each strap.
3. Attach the two straps together with a Chicago screw.
4. Finish each **strap** with a ring end finish at each end.
5. Attach a scissor clip to each ring end.

ADJUSTABLE HOGTIE

Recommended Leather
Use a 6-12oz harness/belt leather and 1" or 1 ¼" straps.

Hardware
4 buckles and keepers, the same width as the strap
8 Chicago screws or rivets
4 Scissor clips
1 O ring, 2-3" diameter

Leather

4 – 8" **buckle straps**.
4 – 12" **end straps**.

Construction
1. Groove all the straps (if desired)
2. Edge the all straps.
3. Give each **end strap** a ring end finish at one end and a belt end finish at the other. For each strap's belt end, punch six holes at 1" intervals, starting 1" from the end.
4. Give each **buckle strap** a buckle end finish using a 1½" fold and a ring end finish using a 1½" fold.
5. Attach a buckle and keeper to each **buckle strap**.
6. Attach the ring end of each **buckle strap** to the front O ring.
7. Attach the ring ends of each **end strap** to a scissor clip.
8. Buckle each **end strap** into a buckle.

BASIC D RING COLLAR

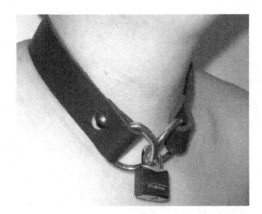

This D Ring collar, also known as a "training collar," can be locked or clipped with a leash.

Recommended Leather

Use a 6-12oz harness/belt leather or use a glued strap made of upholstery leather. The width can range from ¾" to 1 ½". Wider than 1 ½" makes the collar uncomfortable to wear, unless it is contoured into a posture collar.

Hardware

2 – D Rings with an inside width the same as the strap
2 - Chicago Screws or rivets

Measurements

C = Collar measurement – around the throat at the bottom of where the collar should sit.

Leather

1 - **Strap** measuring (C) + 3" finished with a ring end at both ends.

Construction

1. Groove the strap (if desired) and then edge it.
2. Finish the strap with a ring end finish at each end using a 1½" fold.
3. Attach D rings to either end of the strap.

Components of a basic D Ring Collar – 2 Chicago screws, 2 D Rings and one strap.

TWO STRAP BUCKLE COLLAR

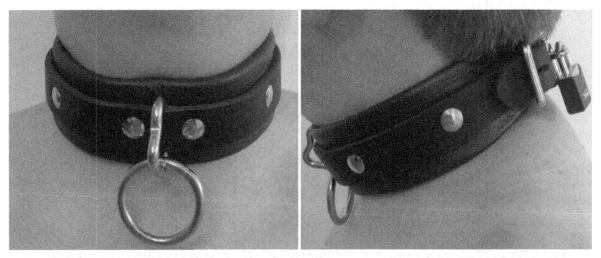

Two strap buckle collar with a loop ring in front. The hunter green inner strap made with a soft garment leather rests against the throat; the 12oz harness leather.outer strap wraps over the inner strap and secures with a locking buckle in back.

Recommended Leather

Use a 6-12oz harness/belt leather or glued strap made of upholstery leather for the straps. The inner strap should be 1¼" or 1½" wide, any wider and the collar will be uncomfortable to wear. The outer strap should be ½" narrower than the inner strap and can be a different color or type of leather than the inner strap.

Hardware

1 buckle (regular or locking) and keeper, same width as outer strap.
5 (or more) Chicago screws or rivets.
1 D Ring or Loop Ring with an inside diameter identical to the outer strap.

Measurements

C = Throat - Measure loosely around the throat at the bottom of where the collar should sit.

Leather

1 **Inner Strap** C inches long
1 **Outer Strap** C+5 inches long

Construction

1. Finish the **outer strap** with a buckle end finish at one end and attach the buckle.
2. Wrap the **inner strap** in a circle so that the ends touch, then wrap the **outer strap** around it so that the buckle is positioned where the ends overlap. Mark the center point of the circle on each strap. Note: if you mark and measure the collar when it is flat, the inner strap will bunch up when it is worn.
3. At the center mark of the **outer strap**, punch holes 5/8" to the left and right of the mark – this will create two holes, 1¼" apart.
4. At the center mark of the **inner strap**, punch holes 1/2" to the left and right of the mark – this will create two holes, 1" apart.
5. Attach the ring with a Chicago screw through each hole.

6. Wrap the **inner strap** in a circle so that the ends touch, then wrap the **outer strap** around it. Mark the points 1/3 and 2/3 of the way between the center and the end of the straps, punch holes through both straps and attach them together with Chicago Screws.
7. Finish the other end of the **outer strap** with a belt end finish so the third hole in the belt end lines up with the buckle when the inner strap ends are touching.

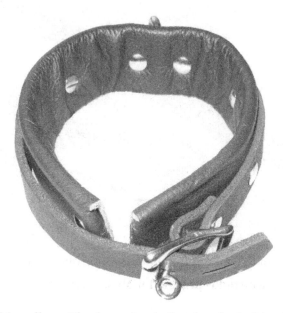

Two strap buckle collar with a loop ring in front and a locking buckle in back.

LEASH

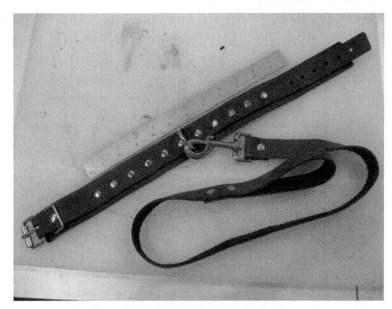

Blue suede riveted collar and matching blue suede leash,

a birthday present for Mistress Musette.

Recommended Leather

Use an 8-12oz harness/belt leather for the leash, ¾" to 1" width is ideal.

I met Mistress Musette and Boy Blue at Leather Leadership Conference Atlanta. Even though his leash was being held by the beautiful Mistress Musette, Boy Blue looked utterly mortified wearing the peach colored leash and collar that they had recently purchased at a local pet store. I found a huge slab of 8oz blue suede in the scrap bin at my local leather store and I made them the blue suede leash and collar set pictured above.

Hardware

1 bolt snap
3 Chicago Screws or rivets

Leather

Strap should be 9" longer than the leash length, e.g. for a 3' leash, use a 3'9" strap.

Construction

1. Finish the strap with a ring end at one end.
2. Attach the strap's ring end through the bolt snap.
3. Make a 7½" fold in the other end of the strap and put Chicago screws 6" and 7" from the fold – they will be ½" and 1½" from the end.

CHEST HARNESS

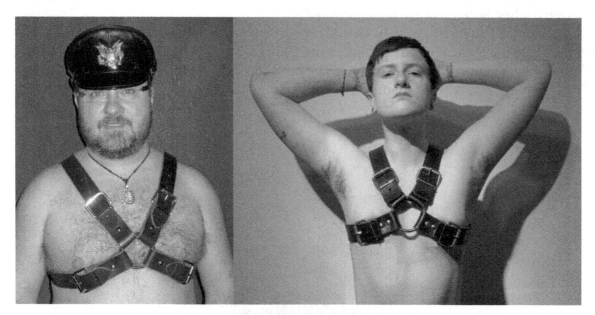

A chest harness with 1 ½" straps can be used to accent the pecs or as a binder.

Description

Chest harnesses are fairly simple to make. Preparing the chest straps in advance (with the ring ends of each strap unfinished) and packaging all the materials together it's possible to have "kits" partially pre-assembled and be able to finish off a custom fit harness in a few minutes.

Recommended Leather

Traditionally made from a 10-12oz harness leather, they can also be made with a glued strap for a softer, more supple feel.

Hardware

4 - buckle and keeper, same width as belt strap
12 - Chicago Screws
2 – O rings that are 2x strap width in diameter (if you are using 1¼" strap, use a 2½" ring, for 1½" strap, a 3" ring.)

Measurements

C - Measure from center of back, tight across the shoulder, across the
chest, under the pectoral muscle or breast and around to the center of the back.

Leather

4 - 6" long **buckle straps**
4 - (C/2)" long **chest straps**

Construction

1. Groove all the straps (if desired)
2. Edge the all straps.

3. Give each **chest strap** a ring end finish at one end and a belt end finish at the other. For each strap's belt end, punch five holes at 3/4" intervals, starting 1" from the end.
4. Give each **buckle strap** a buckle end using a 1¼" fold and a ring end using a 1¼" fold – the ends should touch when both ends are folded inward.
5. Attach a buckle and keeper to each **buckle strap**.
6. Attach the ring end of each **buckle straps** to the front O ring.
7. Attach the ring ends of each **chest straps** to the back O ring.
8. Buckle each chest strap's belt end into its corresponding buckle.

Chest Harness straps and ring connected together.

STOCKINGS

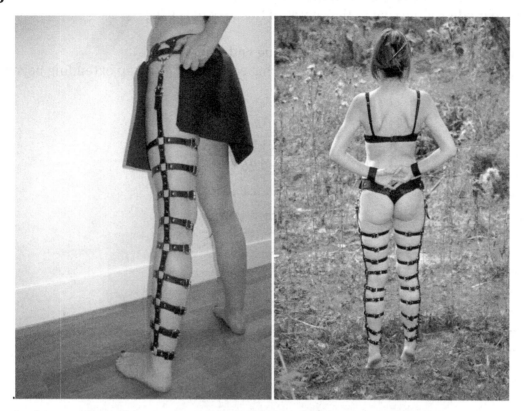

Stockings: rings going up outside of leg (left), buckles centered on back of legs (right)

Recommended Leather

Use fairly stiff garment thickness leather. The leather should have some flexibility to it. Depending on the size of the person, you may choose to use ½"- ¾" width straps – the stockings pictured have 5/8" width straps.

Measurements

Measure from the bottom of the garter belt to the top strap (T) and the top strap to the ankle (A).

Hardware

For each strap, you will need one buckle, one keeper and one ring, diameter twice the strap width (e.g. a 1/2" strap requires a 1" ring.) For these 9 strap stockings, we used 9 1¼" O rings, 9 5/8" buckles and keepers.

You will need an additional buckle, keeper and bolt snap to attach to the belt.

You will need (n) straps with both ends finished with a ring end.

Construction

1. Make the strap of rings first, then run it alongside the outside of the person's leg.
2. At each ring, measure:

A - Around the leg from the rear edge of the ring to the front edge of the ring.
B - From the rear edge of the ring to the center of the back of the leg.

Each **buckle strap** is B + 1 ½" (assuming a ¾" ring end / buckle end.)
Each **belt strap** is (A-B) + 1 ¼" (assuming a ¾" ring end and ¾" of strap extending beyond the buckle.)

A	B	Belt Strap (A-B) + 1 ¼"	Buckle Strap B + 1 ½"
19½	4	16¾	5½
17½	3½	15¼	5.0
15	2½	13¾	4.0
14	3	12¼	4½
12½	2¼	11½	3¾
13½	3	11¾	4½
13	3	11¼	4½
11	2½	10¾	4.0
9	2	8¼	3½

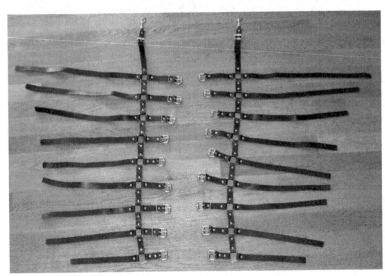

Finished stockings, laid out flat on the floor.

HEAD HARNESS

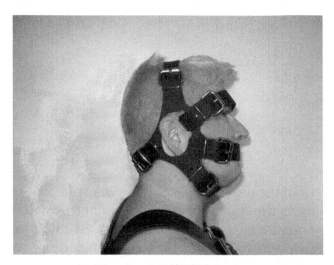

Five Strap Head Harness

Recommended Leather

Use a 6-8oz light harness or belt leather, and 1" straps

Hardware

10 1" buckles (regular or locking) and keepers.
10 Chicago screws or rivets.

Leather

5 **Straps**, M inches long
2 **Head Pieces**

Measurements and Construction

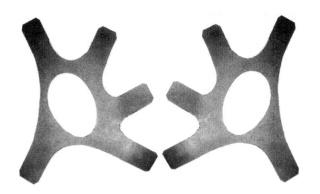

Head pieces should be mirror images of each other.

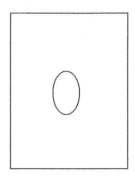 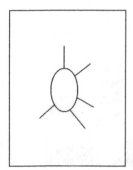 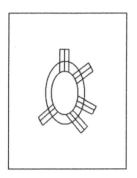

Cut a hole out of a piece of paper large enough to fit over the person's ear.

Hold the paper in place and, using a marker, draw strap lines under the chin, to the corner of the mouth, to the middle of the forehead, to the top of the head and to the back of the neck.

Lay the paper flat on a table and trace a line 1" outside the ear hole. Trace lines ½" left and right of each of the strap lines (yielding a strap width of 1".)

Strap lines should extend 4" from the edge of the ear hole outer circle.

1. Edge the **straps** and **head pieces**.
2. Finish each strap on each **head piece** with a buckle end finish and attach the buckles and keepers to the straps.
3. Starting with the top of the head, do a belt end finish on a **strap** with the first hole 1" from the end and 5 holes at ½" intervals. Buckle the strap at the middle hole, then mark the location of that buckle tongue on the other side, so that both head pieces are held at the same height. Trim and finish the other end of the strap. Repeat for the back of the neck, under the chin, forehead and across the mouth.

The strap across the mouth can be replaced with a bit or a ball gag.

STRAP ON HARNESS

[Photo of Kai and harness]
Strapon Harness

Recommended Leather

For straps, use a 6-8oz light, supple harness leather or make glued/sewn straps with garment or thin upholstery leather. Straps should have 5-10% flexibility, i.e. a 10" sample will flex to 10.5"-11" when it is pulled tight. Automobile or marine upholstery leather is probably the best leather to use for a strapon harness because it is intended to be supple, waterproof and extremely resistant to wear. Avoid using suede or other porous leathers and use latigo only if you have waterproofed it beforehand. Silicone based leather products are probably the best option for waterproofing the leather.

Garment thickness and thin upholstery leather can be sewn in a sewing machine that can handle denim. Perforations in the leather from sewing can cause the leather to rip, so it is recommended that you use a wide stitch to prevent the leather from ripping. Stitching leather is permanent – removing stitches leaves behind holes in the leather.

Double D Ring

Strapon harnesses can be made using either buckles or the double D ring retention strap – under tension, the double D ring holds in place, but once tension is released, the strap comes free.

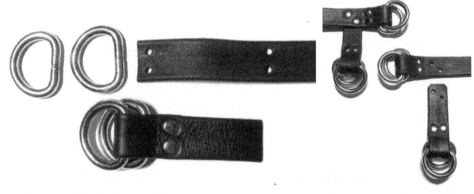

Left: Assembling the double D ring retention strap. Right: strapon harness double D ring hip belt.

Measurements

The two reference points are the **centerpoint**, which is the center of where the dildo should sit when it is worn in the harness and the **hipbone**, which is the point just below the top of the hip bone (the forward most point of the iliac crest.)

H - from the **centerpoint** up to the **hipbone.**
W – Measure from the **centerpoint** up to the **hipbone**, around the back at hipbone level and back to the **centerpoint**.
J – Measure from the **centerpoint** down between the legs and up to the **hipbone** – essentially following the path of the bottom strap of a jockstrap to where it would join the waist strap.

Round Center Pad with O Ring Strap On Harness

The O ring design is a minimal harness that can be used for a variety of cocks. The O ring works well to retain a dildo that doesn't have a wide base. A soft, supple leather and a flexible O ring can be used for a prosthetic cock and balls (also known as a, "packing cock.")

Hardware

4 3/4" buckles and keepers or 8 ¾" D Rings.
8 Chicago screws or rivets.
1¾" diameter O Ring - Metal O rings can be found in a variety of sizes in your local leather store or the heavy thickness Buna-N (also known as Nitrile) O rings be found in large hardware and industrial supply stores.

Leather

2 Front straps, ¾" wide, H+2 inches long
2 Bottom straps, ¾" wide, J – 4 inches long
1 Waist strap, ¾" wide, W – (Hx2) inches long
2 Side straps, ¾" wide, 6 inches long
1 Center Panel, 4-5" diameter circle – use two thicknesses of upholstery leather glued together or a 6-10 oz harness leather with a finished (also called "bonded") back side.

Left: Top straps (top.) Bottom straps (bottom.) Right: Center panel with ¾ inch wide holes.

4. Punch four holes in an X pattern ¾" long, ¼" wide, about ½" from the edge of the **center panel**.
5. Finish both **top straps** with a belt end finish at one end (five holes punched at ½" intervals, starting 1" from the end) and finish the other end with a 1" fold and a button snap. If you are using a double-d ring, do not punch holes in the belt end.
6. Finish the **bottom straps** with a buckle end finish at one end, attach the buckles and then finish the other end with a 1" fold and a button snap. If you are using a double-d ring end, do not finish the bottom straps with a buckle end, instead, cut them 3-4" longer.

7. Insert the snap end of each **top straps** and **bottom straps** through a hole in the **center panel**.
8. Finish the **side straps** with a belt end finish. If you are using a double-d ring, finish the **side straps** with a double-d ring end finish.

Waist strap with the side strap attached through the buckle end.

9. Finish the **waist strap** using a buckle end finish or double-D ring end finish at both ends and attach the **side straps** to each of the buckle ends of the **waist strap**.
10. Attach each buckle end of the **waist strap** to the corresponding **top strap** and attach each **side strap** to the corresponding buckle end of each **bottom strap**.

Triangular Center Strap On Harness

The triangular center strapon harness uses a more supple leather for the center and works well with toys that have a wide base.

Hardware

4 ¾" buckles and keepers or 8 ¾" D Rings.
3 ¾" D or O rings or keepers.
14 small rivets (to attach straps to the center piece)
4 Chicago screws or 16 small rivets (to attach buckles or D rings to the straps.

Leather

2 Top straps, ¾" wide, H+2 inches long
2 Bottom straps, ¾" wide, J – 4 inches long
1 Waist strap, ¾" wide, W – (Hx2) inches long
2 Side straps, ¾" wide, 6 inches long
1 Triangular Center Panel (see below)

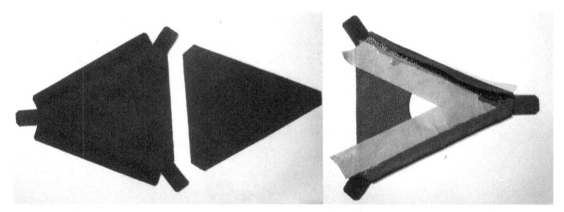

Left: front and back of center piece, right: masked, glued and ready to clamp and dry.

Using the pattern on the following page, cut the front and back pieces and glue them together, clamp and let them dry overnight. After the front and back have dried, use a medium adhesion masking tape to mask the leather and glue the flaps over, clamp and let them dry overnight. One option is to make the center piece without the tabs and substitute 1½"-2" strips of ¾" strap.

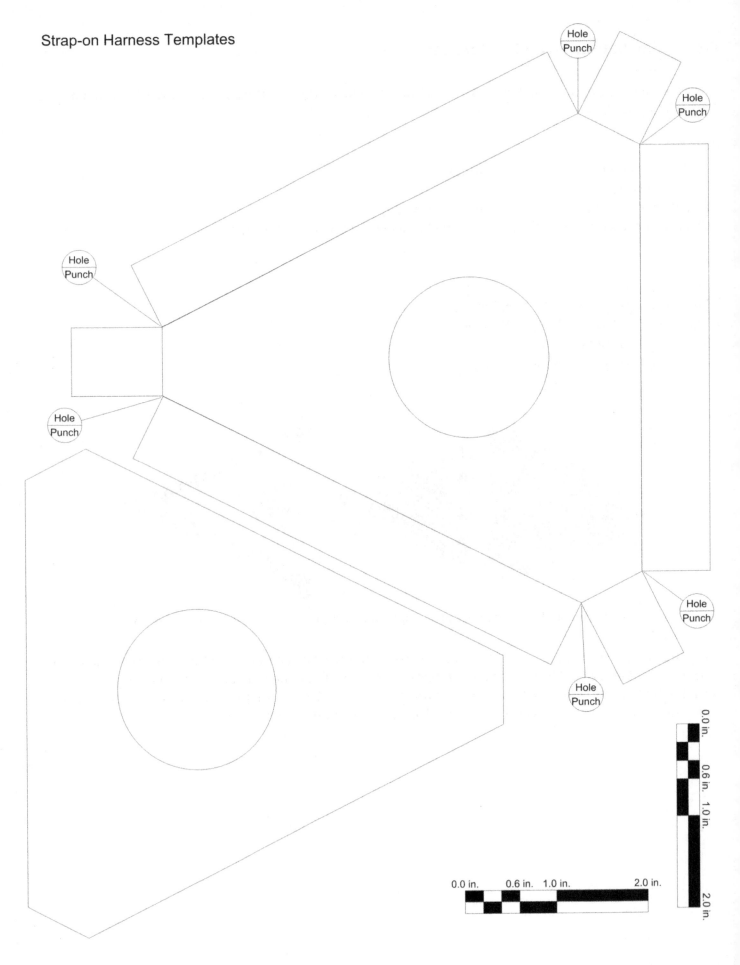

Strap-on Harness Templates

Hole Punch

Hole Punch

Hole Punch

Hole Punch

Hole Punch

Hole Punch

0.0 in.

0.6 in.

1.0 in.

2.0 in.

0.0 in.   0.6 in.   1.0 in.   2.0 in.

Use a D ring at the bottom to provide sufficient space to attach both bottom straps.

There are several options for attaching rings – ¾" O rings, D rings or even rectangular keepers will all work well. Use two small rivets to distribute the tension more evenly – a single rivet is more likely to tear or pull through the leather. When punching holes for the rivets, use the smallest hole possible to avoid the leather stretching and allowing the rivet to pop out.

Cutting the hole a 1¾" diameter is the "industry standard" for the center hole in strapon harnesses. Options for cutting the hole are to use circular Arch Punch (they can be quite expensive,) a razor blade and a circular guide, or a circle cutter. Circle cutters are available from fabric and craft stores.

Hole cutting options – l to r 1¾" circular arch punch, craft knife and circular guide, circle cutter.

1. Finish the **side straps** with a belt end finish. If you are using a double-d ring, finish the **side straps** with a double-d ring end finish.
2. Finish both **top straps** with a belt end finish at one end (five holes punched at ½" intervals, starting 1" from the end) and a ring end finish at the other end. If you are using a double-d ring, finish the top strap with a double-d ring finish, and attach the side strap to the top strap (see photo.) Attach the top straps to the top of the center panel.
3. Finish the **bottom straps** with a buckle end finish at one end and a ring end finish at the other end. If you are using a double-d ring end, do not finish the bottom straps with a buckle end, instead, cut them 3-4" longer. Attach the **bottom straps** to the bottom of the center panel.

Waist strap with the side strap attached through the buckle end.

4. Finish the **waist strap** using a buckle end finish and attach the **side straps** to each of the buckle ends of the **waist strap.** If you are using a double-D ring end finish, do not do anything to the either end of the **waist strap.**
5. Attach each buckle end of the **waist strap** to the corresponding **top strap** and attach each **side strap** to the corresponding buckle end of each **bottom strap**.

SEVEN GATES OF HELL

This is a very intimidating looking piece of BDSM gear that is surprisingly easy to make.

Most of the guys that I know who own one say, "It doesn't fit. Most Gates of Hell are made, "one size fits all," while men aren't made to the same specifications.

The first ring goes around the base of the penis and the testicles – pull the scrotum through the ring, then push each testicle through the ring, then push the soft penis through the ring (TGIF stands for, "Testicles Go In First.") The remainder of the rings go around the shaft of the penis.

Recommended Leather

Use a relatively soft garment or upholstery leather strap, ½" is probably the best width.

Hardware

7 – O Rings of varying sizes (see Measurements and Construction below.)
6 – Small rivets

Measurements

To get a custom fit, measure the penis when it is erect. Measure the length of the top of the erect penis from base to tip (L) and tight around the base of the penis and testicles (D1.) Starting ¾" from the base, measure the circumference of the shaft in increments (½" is the minimum recommended distance) increments (D2 through D7 and possibly more.) The better endowed may wind up with a 9 Gates of Hell, some may have only 5 Gates of Hell.

Leather

1 - **Strap** measuring (L X 2) + 1", however you can add additional straps for 2, 3 or even 4 strap versions. Be aware that adding additional straps may require increasing the ring diameter slightly to accommodate the space taken up by the straps inside the rings.

Construction

1. Edge the strap(s.)
2. Fold the leather in a loop with ½" of each end overlapping the other.
3. Punch holes at each increment.
4. Starting with the loop opposite the ends, insert the corresponding ring, then set a rivet in the hole behind the ring to hold it in place.
5. Repeat this process until all the rings have been placed.

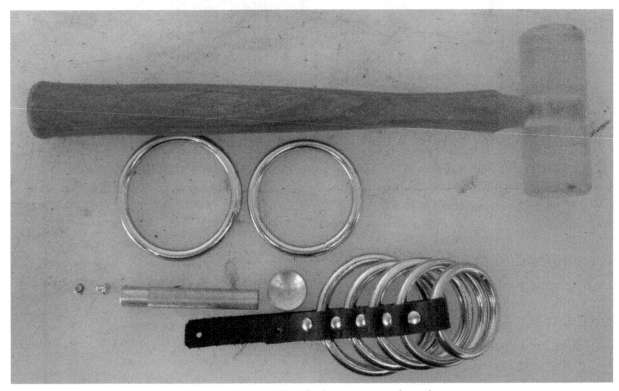

Seven Gates of Hell almost completed.

FLOGGERS

From top to bottom: Purple flogger, 9" handle with 4 strand braided wrap, with 18 falls made from 3oz leather, each ½" wide and 18" long. Brown flogger, 10" spiral wrap handle, with 28 falls made from 6oz leather, each ¾" wide and 22-26" long. Black flogger, 8" handle with 4 strand braided wrap, with 20 falls made from 8oz leather, each ½" wide and 19" long. Red flogger, 9" handle with 4 strand braided wrap, with 30 falls made from 6oz leather, each ½" wide and 19" long.

Parts of a Flogger

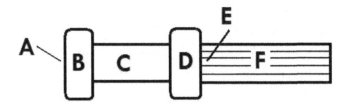

A – Back Cap, B – Back Wrap, C – Handle, D – Front Wrap, E – Front Cap, F - Falls

The Average Flogger

The "average" flogger has a handle diameter of approximately ¾", handle length of 6-9 inches and falls of 12-18 inches. The handle length is usually about ½ the length of the falls or 1/3 of the overall length of the flogger, e.g. an 18" flogger will have a 6" handle and 12" falls. The weight of the handle should be greater than or equal to the weight of the falls so that the flogger feels balanced.

Leather

You will need several types of leather for your flogger. The front cap leather should be garment thickness leather that matches the color of the falls. The handle padding should be 2-6oz spongy leather that matches the color of the handle wrap. The handle wrap should be garment thickness for a four strand wrap and garment to chap thickness for a spiral wrap. To make a flogger like the black or red flogger in the previous photograph, you will need:

One 9"x19" piece of leather to cut into falls
One 4"x9" piece of leather to use for padding
Two 4-5 foot long 3/8" lacing for a single-pass gaucho knot
Two circular pieces of leather (1¾" and 2" diameter) to make end caps
Two 4" long, 1 ½" wide strips of strap leather (un-edged belt end scraps.)

Flogger Falls

Determine the desired width and length of a single fall. Add 1" to the desired length of a fall to get the total **fall length**. Multiply the desired number of falls by the width of an individual fall to get the **overall width** of the **fall piece**. The flogger pictured above has twenty ¾" wide, 18" long falls, which required a 15" wide, 19" long piece of leather.

It is sometimes easier to create and weigh the handle and then cut the falls so that the weights match. An alternate technique is, after cutting the falls, weigh them and then add weight to the handle. The best option for doing so is to insert lead discs or washers into the end of the handle before gluing on the end cap.

HOW TO GET STING OR THUD FROM FLOGGER FALLS		
	Sting	**Thud**
Leather Thickness	Thin	Thick
Width	Narrow (1/4")	Wide (3/4")
Finish	Smooth (Wax finish)	Rough (Suede or Oil Tan)
Edges/Tips	Sharp Corners	Rounded
Flexibility	Stiff	Supple

Cutting Flogger Falls

1. Using a small diameter leather punch, make a line of holes 1" from the handle end of the fall leather that are "fall width" apart.

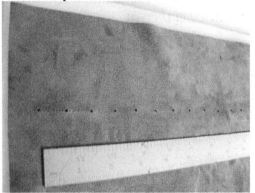

A line of holes ¾" apart, 1" from the handle end of the fall leather.

2. Mark the opposite end of the fall piece at the same interval.

3. With a metal edged ruler and a fresh single edged razor blade or a rotary cutter, using the hole and the mark as guides, cut from the hole to the end of the fall piece.

4. After cutting each fall, flip it up out of the way so that it does not get nicked or cut in the next pass.

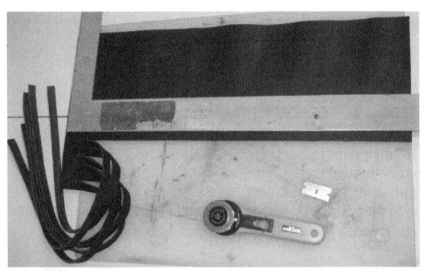

After cutting a fall, flip it out of the way.

Handle Core

"Handle cores? I've used everything: wooden dowel, broom handles, mop handles, wood curtain rod, metal pipe, plastic pipe. If it's round and leather will stick to it, I've probably used it." -Flogger vendor at Mid-Atlantic Leather

The best way to make a handle core is to cut an 8" long, ½" or ¾" inside diameter piece of metal pipe and sand the outside with #40 sandpaper. Use a 9" piece of ½" or ¾" wood dowel that fits snugly into the pipe, coat it with epoxy glue, glue it inside the pipe, and leave 1" of the dowel sticking out the end.

Handle End Caps

**Cap with a circle of holes (left.) Cutting triangles from the cap to make flaps (center.)
Final cap with 8 flaps (right.)**

Using garment weight leather with a color that matches the handle braid or the falls, do the following:

1. Cut a circular cap of leather with a diameter 1" greater than the end.
2. Using a 1/16" diameter leather punch, punch holes in a circle with a diameter 1/8"-1/4" larger than the end diameter.
3. Make triangular cuts from the holes to make flaps to attach to the sides.
4. Glue the cap to the end, fold the flaps down and use rubber bands to hold the cap in place.

Cap rubber banded in place (left.) Cap after being glued in place (right.)

Handle Padding

Wrap the handle core with a thick, spongy piece of leather that matches the color of the handle braid – this wrap will pad the handle and will disguise any imperfections in the handle braiding. This wrap should match up evenly and not overlap. Wrap the leather in rubber bands and allow the glue to set overnight.

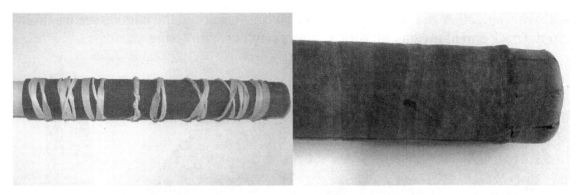

Wrap the handle padding in rubber bands and let the glue set overnight (left)
Closeup of handle wrap and end cap(right)

BRAIDING THE HANDLE

There are an amazing (and bewildering) variety of ways to braid a handle and it is the most time-consuming part of making a flogger. We will cover the two most common, the spiral wrap and the 4 strand braid.

Spiral Wrap Braid (top.) Four Strand Braid (bottom.)

FOUR STRAND BRAIDED HANDLE

Braiding from the back of the handle toward the front gives the best results – the first inch of braid, which is most likely to show flaws, will be hidden under the end cap.

Using 4 strips of leather that are at least ¼ the circumference of the handle, secure their ends to the back end of the handle with a rubber band or with string.

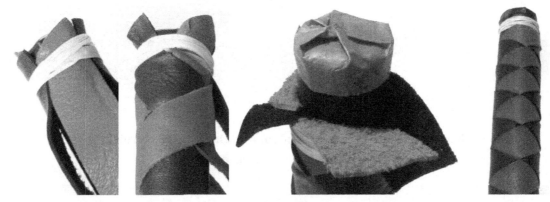

Four strand braid front and rear are black, left and right are red (left.) Start of braid showing left over center and rear pulled around to front (center left.) Rubber band pulled down and strips peeled back ½" for gluing (center right) Finished four strand braid (right.)

1. Pull the left strip over the center strip.
2. Pull the rear strip around from the back, under the right strip and over the left strip.
3. Pull the right strip around the back under the front strip and over the back strip.
4. Continue the braiding down the handle, wrapping two strands then rotating until the braid is complete.
5. Use a rubber band over the end of the braid to keep it from unwrapping.
6. Pull the rubber band back about ½", glue the strips into position and secure the glued strips with a rubber band.
7. Allow the glue to set overnight.

SPIRAL WRAPPED HANDLE

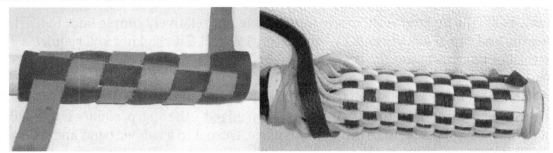

A spiral wrap around the handle core requires an even number of slits in the wrap (left)
The pattern when the lace is twice as wide as the slit width (right.)

1. To make a spiral wrapped handle, cut a strip of leather that is long enough to wrap in a spiral and completely cover the handle. Add another 1/4 - 1/3 to the overall length to allow for the loss due to weaving.
2. Cut a rectangular strip of leather that is as long as the handle and that wraps completely around the handle.
3. Cut an even number of evenly spaced slits in the wrap, leaving ¼" at the top and bottom to hold the piece together. To do this, use your smallest hole punch and punch holes at the chosen interval ¼" from the edge of the piece, then use a metal edged ruler and a single edged razor blade and cut a straight line from hole to hole.
4. Using a rubber band, secure the top of the wrap to the top of the handle. Starting opposite the side where the edges of the leather meet, insert the lace into the slits in an over/under pattern pulling the lace consistently tight throughout the process. Use a fid or knitting needle to push the laces together – consistent tension and pressure is crucial to ensuring that the lacing looks good.
5. Once the lacing is complete, remove the rubber bands and apply leather glue to the ¼" edge at the top and bottom, glue the ends of the lace underneath the wrap and secure with rubber bands.
6. Allow the glue to set overnight.

Parts of a spiral wrapped handle: wrap with even number of slits and the lace.

SINGLE PASS GAUCHO KNOT

The single pass gaucho knot is an impressive looking but relatively simple knot to use for braiding the end cap of a flogger. A 1½" diameter, 1½" tall Gaucho knot will require a 3/8" wide lace about five feet long.

Wrap the handle end in a 1"-1½" wide collar of 8-12oz leather – this is a great way to use belt scraps. Use a piece of leather that <u>has not been edged</u> – the sharp, square edges will help hold the wrap in place. Glue the collar in place, wrap it in a rubber band and let the glue set overnight.

Use lace that is approximately the same width as the gap between the handle core and the distance to the end cap.

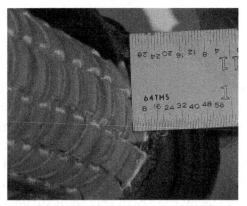

Measuring the gap between the handle wrap and the outer edge of the cap.
This measured to 20/64", which meant that we used 5/16" lace.

Start by wrapping the braid once around the collar, looping the lace so that it wraps over the top and bottom edges of the collar. On the second wrap, cross over the first wrap on the top edge of the collar.

Wrapping once around the collar (left.) Start of second wrap (center.) Cross over the first wrap on the top edge of the collar (right.)

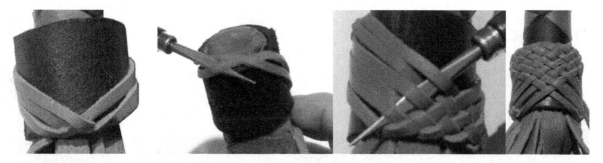

Lace going under the first lace, over the second and over the collar edge (left.) The fid shows the path of the lace on top of the collar (center left.) Fid shows the path of the lacing alternating over/under pattern (center right.) The Gaucho knot builds (right center.)

Pull the lace down to the bottom edge of the collar and run it under the first lace, over the second lace and around the bottom edge of the collar. Wrap the lace around to the top edge and repeat the pattern: pull it under the first lace on the bottom and over the second lace. Continue wrapping around the collar, alternating over/under as you wrap.

After braiding the gaucho knot, trim the lace ends to ¾" length. Use masking tape to cover the end of the handle up to the edge of the gaucho knot. Apply a liberal coat of leather glue to the lace ends and then push them under the lace and under the edge of the collar.

Trimming the lace ends (left.) Handle wrapped with masking tape (center.) Tucking the lace under the collar (right.)

FLOGGER ASSEMBLY

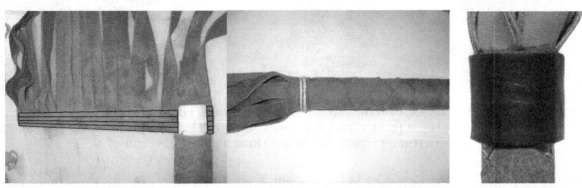

Apply glue to the 1" attachment strip (marked with horizontal lines above, left.) Staple and
then roll the falls onto the handle, then secure them in place while the glue sets (center.)
After the glue has set, wrap a collar around the falls (right.)

1. After all the falls have been cut, spread glue across the 1" attachment strip, then roll the
   falls onto the handle core. Keep the attachment strip taut as you roll so that the falls are
   held tight against the handle.
2. Use string or rubber bands to secure the glued strip and allow the glue to set overnight.
3. Use a wood screw that is ½ the diameter of the dowel plus falls and screw the falls to
   the dowel.
4. Make a "collar" using a 1½" wide scrap of 8-12 oz belt leather around the falls and the
   end of the handle. Glue this scrap into place over the falls, positioning it so that it
   covers the holes at the bottom of the falls and also covers the join between the handle
   wrap and the falls. To prevent the falls from getting glue on them, wrap the falls in a
   plastic bag and secure with masking tape (the blue painter's tape is ideal because
   inexpensive masking tape can be acidic and leave marks on leather.)
5. Allow the glue to set overnight.
6. If the handle diameter differs from the fall diameter, use scrap leather glued into place
   as a shim to fill the gap before attaching the collar.
7. Wrap the collar with a single pass gaucho knot, using lace that is approximately the
   same width as the distance between the handle and the edge of the collar.

Thanks

I'd like to thank my boy Hobbit for all her support during the time that it took to write this book, Henry for his help and pointing me in the right direction for starting this project, Ernesto for inspiring the first piece of leather work, Andie for being such a well prepared boi, Jaison for showing me what creative things can be done with just one leather punch (and a hammer), Monica for all her help and showing me what amazing leather work can be done with a box cutter, Ash for all the help at my first Folsom Street Fair, Parker for being a such a great model and muse, Kenneth for his fabulous fashion sense, Aaron for liking the fact that the hood has no vent holes, Mo for looking great in gear and for motivating me to stay at the workbench, Lee for looking so damn good in gear I've made, Leo for instigating, Tia and William for sharing their knowledge of equestrian gear, Skeeter for inspiring the idea for the book, Diamond Jack for stepping up and for making a leather tie look really good in front of such a big audience, Texas John for helping me break my first flogger, Mistress Musette and Blue for inspiring me to cut into that hunk of blue suede, Tria for a wonderful weekend and some great boot work, Roxy for all her editorial work, Travis for some excellent photography , Sparrow for some really helpful braiding geek sessions, all the people who bought leather gear to help Hobbit during her year as International Ms Leather, the folks at Fetlife.Com and LeatherWorker.Net and all the members of Seattle Men in Leather for helping get this show on the road.

Made in the USA
Middletown, DE
28 January 2020